Ledger

winner of the IOWA POETRY PRIZE

Ledger

SUSAN WHEELER

University of Iowa Press Ψ IOWA CITY

University of Iowa Press, Iowa City 52242

Printed in the United States of America

Design by Richard Hendel

http://www.uiowa.edu/uiowapress

The University of Iowa Press is a member of
Green Press Initiative and is committed to preserving
natural resources.

Printed on acid-free paper

Library of Congress Cataloging-in-Publication Data

Wheeler, Susan, 1955–.

    Ledger / by Susan Wheeler.

        p.   cm.—(Iowa poetry prize)

     ISBN 0-87745-927-4 (pbk.)

     I. Title.   II. Series.

   PS3573.H43465L43   2005

   811'.54—dc22   2004058021

05 06 07 08 09 P 5 4 3 2 1

for David

Having been a tenant long to a rich Lord,

 Not thriving, I resolved to be bold,

 And make a suit unto him, to afford

A new small-rented lease, and cancell th' old.

—George Herbert, "Redemption"

They did not understand that even an economic world order cannot be built on merely economic foundations.

—Arnold J. Toynbee, *A Study of History*

Contents

Ledger

Loss Lieder

It's an icebox
missing freon,
elevator
that's kaput.
It's a danger
in the stashbox,
fast upon us
citigrade.
Lay your head
on radiators,
drive the needle
through the vein;
I'll be here when
you're no longer,
opal midnight
my refrain.
I'll sing it when
you're mentioned
if the cost is
not too great,
and if I haven't
met you coming
toward us
in the haze.

Proper Return

That Been to Me My Lives Light and Saviour

Purse be full again, or else must I die. This is the wish
the trees in hell's seventh circle lacked, bark ripped by monstrous dogs,
bleeding from each wound. We see them languid there,
the lightened purse a demon drug. *Less, less.*

At the canal, the dog loops trees in a figure eight —
a cacophony of insects under sun. A man against a tree nods off.

Let there be no sandwich for the empty purse.
Let there be no raiment for someone skint.
Let blood run out, let the currency remove.
Let that which troubles trouble not.

My father in the driveway. Legs splayed behind him. Pail beside him.
Sorting handfuls of gravel by shade and size. One way to calm
a pecker, compensate for stash. *Dad!* I lied.

The man shifts by the tree and now grace is upon him.
The slant of sun picks up the coins dropped by travelers and — lo! —
grace enables him to see. The demon dog fresh off an eight barks, too,
standing, struck by the man, by the coins, barks at their glare;
the man reaches in scrim at the glint in the light and thinks *Another
malt.* The flesh is willing, the spirit spent,

                                        the cloud passes over —
relief is not what you think, not the light. Regard the barking
dog now tugging at the dead man's leg becoming bark.

You be my life, you be my heart's guide,
you be the provision providing more,
you be the blood — stanch the sore! —
you be failing

proportion (mete) . . .

Steward of gravel squints up at the girl who is me.
What? defensively. Out of the east woods, a foaming raccoon spills.
Palmolive executive? Palmolive customer? Palm's stony olives
                            on the embankment of limestone or soapstone or
shale. Leg of the man clamped in the dog's mouth. Mouth
of the man open and unmoved. Voice of the man:

Three dolls sat within a wood, and stared, and wet when it rained
into their kewpie mouths. They were mine to remonstrate to the
trees at large, the catalpas and the fir, the sugar maples in the
glade turning gold. To each is given, one doll began, so I had
to turn her off. Consider how it was for me —

Flash of the arrow and the foam falls down. Three balletists
ignoring pliés bound onto the long lawn and its canalward
slope. I am underwater and they haze in the light,

                                             mouth

but do not sound. In the arrow's blink they start.

Decimal as piercing of the line —
Table as imposition of the grid —
Sum as heuristic apoplex —
Columns in honeysuckle cents — or not.

Just this transpired. Against a tree I swooned and fell, and
water seeped into my shoe, and a dream began to grow in me.
Or despair, and so I chose the dream. And while I slept,
I was being fed, and clothed, addressed — as though awake
with every faculty, and so it went. Then: blaze, blare of sun

after years uncounted, and synesthesia of it and sound,
the junco's chirp and then the jay's torn caw, arc
of trucks on the distant interstate, your *what the fuck*
and then her call. Beside me, pinned to a green leaf,
in plastic and neat hand, a full account. I had indeed still
lived, and been woke for more. So, weeping then, I rose.

Roanoke and Wampumpeag

Child, entering Ye Olde Trading Post, takes the pegs upon the walls
For trees, fingers the beaded doll in buckskin dress, a moccasin,

A square of maple sugar maple leaf, small imprint of a fingernail
In its clear window. She wants the Minnesota charm in green,

Six of ten thousand lakes in silver raised, Babe the Blue Ox and her
Mate. REAL! CAN OF WORMS! a label states; another, on a bow

And arrows stapled into cellophane: APACHE ARROWHEADS,
AUTHENTIQUE. Dread of parents, parked, smoking, in the lot.

Piecework of the quiet shade. Piecework of the whoosh of trees
Blowing beyond log walls, adults murmuring over turquoise rings,

Low radio, woman propped with *The Making of a President*
Open in her hands. The child calculates the thieving odds, balks.

A brother, suddenly. *Come ON*. The dollar buys four old-tyme sticks,
Swirled barber poles in green and brown, horehound-hard and stale,

Each a member's of the family, their car on gravel moving out, trunk
To traders and the totem pole, behind the ghastly, grinning cow.

The Green Stamp Book

Child in the thick of yearning. Doll carted and pushed
like child. The aisles purport opportunities —

looking up, the women's chins, the straight rows
of peas and pretzels, Fizzies' foils, hermetic

boxes no one knows. *I'll get it!* What thing therein
 — bendy straws, powder blue pack Blackjack gum —

will this child fix upon? On TV, women with grocery carts
careen down aisles to find expensive stuff. Mostly,

this means meat. This, then, is a life. This, a life
that's woven wrong and, woven once, disbraided, sits

like Halloween before a child, disguised in its red
Santa suit, making its lap loom the poppy field

Dorothy wants to bed. *Can I have* and the song's begun.
O world spotted through more frugal legs. O world.

Carnival

Boy in lit din — trailing tickets in strings, a man on his hand —
tilts at the red poles, dots, rainbows in kliegs; tilts past

rickety gates manned by bent men, men bent into bars like the man
with the boy bends to bars, too; tilts as a t-shirt shoves and dissolves.

Boy blinking in noise, with coupon trails, veers at the hand out to
Wipeout near Yo Yo and Claw; Graviton, Zipper, Chaos, Rock and Roll —

this: major ride row. Slime Buckets. Orbiter. Night with its
sear of crayon through ink. Boy in the spill of shapes liquid at night.

Motherfucker give 'em to me, the man's the boy's master and
his own dive he feints, bending, too. *This ain't TV.* Pulled up to

concessions. Stopped straight under white. Major Ride Row,
its Fire Ball, Tornado, zipped out of reach, sees the man on the end

of the boy levy a string for a carton of drinks. *It's not free.*
Would that a wave from the night past the trees take him, take him,

far away from me: this they both wish from their roiling seas,
in dins of temptations, in the slugs from the noise both would be.

Doubled Indemnity

Then those same pendant profits, which the spring
And Easter intimate, enlarge the thing . . .
— George Herbert, "Lent"

Late twentieth century, lower Fifth Avenue.
Cars spurting in the pendant day.

                Bell over a jeweler's door. Girl.
                Tumble of hair. Packet

from a purse and out, and open.
Fall of gold rings on glass case.

                Ten karats ten karats — gold's
                homogeneity in kind.

Scandal of the *particularity*
of Christ, she said,

                ten karats ten templed his
                own fingers, too.

Ten it will get you. Bell
over a jeweler's door. Cars

                spurting in the pendant day.

Each's Cot an Altar Then

. . . from the service of self
alone . . .

grasses in low wind high sun

(streamers of starlings)

Joseph hauling the leg with his hands, corn stubble to stalk, horizon no house —

Low animal flash in the riot of leg —

all such good works as thou hast prepared for us to walk in

This one request I make if it mean foot or glove
Repair, deplete the debt as I am out of love

carrion   calumny

and come into the field of blade poplars glinting,
leg pulled like a cart on the mule of the man
grasshopper of cropduster sprawled in the sun
desperate pastor all yield green pan

                                        Limb lost? Likely.
                                        Undone? Likely.

                Let us grant it is not amiss

who bears the Count Chocula shipment up
who razors the retractable in the joint
who sings the bass of Anthony
who cries for mercy in the placid field,

                        far now to go.

                        to reel the streets at noon —
                so great weight in his lightness —

So. Bike at door.
On it. Avenue
of the Americas   (against traffic)
a stream.
        The
spareribs hot against
his knees.

              fiduciary re
              no sib
              ability re-
              spond dis
              Eisenhower, Eisenhower

                                sty

pend   sur

          plus one is
              x, solve for.   solve

          .

vent

A kind of Mamie-dress, that's right, with the bodice —
no — you'd need darts here first. But that kind
of print —

kind of

a clear light above Joseph and his leg and the dry dry stalks and the clatter he
   makes

seek a proper return for our labor

Short Shrift

I was at and about everything, nodding through the mall lot,
cutting through the yard with quick, light steps.

When the rains came,
they left the hillside
and moved to the high ground
where a quilt scrap sustained them
in late, dark readings from
Isaiah, bright
                    "and they

regard the objectivity of the market as a disguise for an abdication of values
and of intellectual dependence"   Wm Pfaff, 1981

In this house, objects
operate optimally.
The log on the fire is
seasoned to flame,
the chips in the basket
Olestra cramp not.

"You're hurting my arm."

—— and then the jingle wings in
—— striated penna of the ostrich
— O noble heart,

ponder thy end.

On the floor we saw the pigs
in space routine:
Jack whirling in the zigzag of the
rise, the fall, the buy high,
sell.
Bodies doubled over slush underfoot
of the tape,
loss-evidence,
white shit.

He got the newsprint spread about
So he ha, so he ha
He got the newsprint spread about
So he ha

the signature inscription, the sport-fuck after boot scoot, the U.S. of

He got the newsprint spread about
An he hacking, spitting low
He expectorating upon the news

Give me that core lone tearing. Rest your head. Put it here.

"It's just routine."

I will be brief.
Upon his death
They felt relief.

A delight exacting

The night and the stars and the window
The sigh and the gown and the fiddle
The calling to hymn and from sorrow
jumping   gel O

"Let's put the dutiful graduate student thing away, ok? Dazzle as summarily
as the theorists. Our ducks in a row. No ~~wine~~ whine."

At dawn their path
took sea side by the bethel,
up Guinevere
along the Pathmark lot,
through the early fields,
the sun rising red
and hung.

"Thank you, I prefer to stand."

Tyvek Bruce Willis Buffalo Bertelsman Turtle Wax Tiger Balm
Nickel Cadmium Postgraduate Ice Cube Waldrop
Exile Witness Nike Iowa Snapple Foucault, The Sands
Browning Tradition, Hejinian, Bly — SKU, ADP, BAP
Time-Warner, Ted Turner, The Favorite Poem Project, the Oulipo, the Fed
Independent Cinema, Mrs. B's, Miss Lou, Reds

lemon trees tennis bracelet desert   highway

She had been pinged, like the
pillar in a pinball, by the die
of god. Lit in the klieg of a
sign. Stung by repletion &
furious in sin, a monolith of
infirmity washed clean. A
domino undone by the smear
on its back. Left to contend
in the swale of her city's
chokeweeds and strife, she had
truck in sinew, in tooth
and in tongue, with divinity,
raw. Then it passed.

"Had killed the whole carload of them."

crawed fish

bone

When you get your job
in the powder factory
I'll macrame your mask.

I don't want to spread it around.

Naturally. The finitude of the body! The demands of the soul!
Did you hear about the butter?

The ironic caw of the crows flapping past to the Farmer's Corn —

and salt

and pepa

Naugahyde
TV room
Overhead glare
Child crumpled in love

Three dollars fifty cents a celebrity magazine, buck fifty a caffé latté on sale.
A twenty and change for a belt with D rings, a fin for the xeroxing and mail.
Seven twenty the lipstick, thirteen coins the handouts, Susan B. a scone, stale.

My consumerism: Rerelease   *India*
                           Rerelease   *India*

India: a meronym of that dark winter, cold, on foot, Chicago, the ta-*da* the grace

"You've got the wrong man."

If memory mimed dreaming then I would have you here again.
You would be laughing gem-like, praising Republicans.
Ailing, sipping sours, you would be diffident.
O that your Curwensville had found
A way to harbor you!
And that I hadn't spent the pound
I'd saved to honor you.

The plot in the account books
The sermon in the billboard
The dark night of the statement
Mercy in direct deposit

lights on, nobody home

We doctor shoes
attend the dyeing
heel them
save their soles
in Red Bank, New Jersey

"Oh, by the way, just one more thing."

They came from a woolly world and they wanted an exact, undisclosed freedom.
They wore small hairpins and carried their sons close to their chests.
Before they came, they felt they had failed at understanding the outside and the inside.
What they found was a replica of nature.
What they found was menace recollected in tranquility.
What they found came in small pine coffins.
They were eager to undertake difficulty and they were eager to repel the consequences.
They wanted danger to have names they knew.
They came from resplendent churches made of wicker.
They roasted hens.
They built shelters, each with an oak plank frame.
They understood that a gathering of hearts meant for — by now! — few words.

"Take a seat."
"Thank you, I prefer to stand."

Surfeit

Hand, Mouth, Market

In any structure, you can obtain cable service,
you can connect a flat-screen television, you
can watch the Yankees and the Mariners as
prelude to a subway series. You can remove
a bottle of beer from a refrigerator. You can
make a bed. The structure is arbitrary, it comes
with a salary, the eaves peaked or the roof shovel-
ready in the snow season, the gutters full of twigs
or covered with small runners, caps really,
to protect the runnels, the water chutes, something
not invented by Disney but American nonetheless,
uncoppered in the tenting of our depots, where
you can stare from a kitchen window at a dog
devouring a flea and then shitting on your lawn.

Into this, stride loved ones not unforgotten
in the mix of peat moss and cereal, fenders,
and the rhetorical hum of the baseboard heat,
and you can hear them calling you from the front
room to come quickly, see the skunk in the road,
and you can ignore them. Other prerogatives
of a paycheck include sleeping in on a Sunday.
You can also — and here we come back to the
refrigerator again — pillage supplies for a snack.
Above, in the beat of the sky, Vanna on the
Hollywood Squares stares back. Bumps on the
bark of the maple concern you by and by.

Into this you can introduce debt. Dots on the
screen can feather all your expectations
for rodeos and whatnot, the structure arbitrary,

a composite cribbed from vagaries such as
typically visit upon our scenes. The grass
growing drier in the drama of accounting. Punks
you believe the neighbors' kids to be come
to your door. Harry meets Sally again and again.
Braked or full speed it is a kind of locking.
But when you deploy your own self and those
selves of your loved ones with out, out,
red birds on soft slate can menace, too.

On the lawn, on the tarmac, beneath a bridge,
you can run the wires off of errant lines, you
can choose the indictment that is Seinfeld, a
car, or spittle the screen with vituper.
A flatness results, be it American or Mills,
General Mills, General Foods, elves and
Jemimahs and so forth, on to Jeannies and
Samanthas and O — O that you not be left so
alone when the power line fails! Buck up and
tell it, buck up and tell them, the sores on your
hide hide nothing, the stenciling on the door
does nothing —— you can walk, you can wake
by the side of the road, a friend to critters there,
and man.

Good Goods

. . . all that a man . . . discourseth in his spirit
is nothing but merchandise.
— John Wheeler, *A Treatise in Commerce*

Having trafficked in ideas, they turned to birds, and
soon depleted stocks in quails, purple finches,
black-capped chickadees, goldfinches, brown
thrashers, orioles. Surprise, at the fridge: Hilal,
looking for her thimble. *A pity.* Then they turned to
cornerstones — to this and that, mainly to town
halls; and despite their efforts, supply engulfed
demand. Marx hadn't helped. One hundred and
sixty billion was the usual ballpark on tie-ins for the
pint-sized. They tried figurines, energy shakes,
cruises, whales, and tulle. Brian yawned in the
boardroom. The girl Story: "If it fits, take six."
Trumpet call — mouth cupped upon an ear — but
enslaved did they remain. Booted up to tacos at a
drive-in. And they found courtship a sudden object
of the marketplace. Benjy: *This language sucks.*
But what to substitute? Lights, blinking, harbor at
night, the boats lapped by sea — even these they
tried. Bill, in his lair, malt liquor. And so, coming
down from the agora, they wept from exhaustion
and despair. And so, they filtered apparitions,
through dermatologist and butcher, and wept,
despairing of return.

Charity Must Abide Call for Ancient Occupation

Red barn, still house, shimmering heat.
Brown barn, air in rain, green smell.
I climbed the hill to volunteer my hands:
O works that we may walk in.
The rodent's toe in the pinecone cell,
the brackish bag with its damp wax gel,
beside the fence links, glinting.

One was spending one hundred thirteen degrees
supporting the basic initiative,
in his trailer, terminally wounded in Congress,
waiting for sunset so he could sound alarms about its ability
to spend hours putting temporary fences,
implementing, nondiscriminatory,
not only his sheep when it comes to gays but,
when it comes to all their dogs in holes they had dug
to religious faiths, under trailers,
to groups providing government-funded, blistering heat.

And one, Solomon, solemn one, puled,
She, initiate in the knowledge of Him,
co-creator in His works,
I determined to take her to live with me,
for if we want riches in life, what be greater bounty
than the knowledge that triggers all things?

I waited on that corner until the yelling began,
the sharp horn, the crumpling steel ——
until the songbirds swooped in like carrion,
into the funnel of charitable provisions,
sounding the alarm in a surfeit of ours,

initiates, faith based in moneylenders' lairs.
I credited their flight. Wrung charity.
But the wing flapping went on in the heat.

In the hour before sunrise the wet & swift wings ceased.
Should there be, I thought, a mandible for each?
A Dolly for each Sofia? Faith entering the breach?
Still air, expectant, dark. The legalese.
From one I will expect, before earth us takes,
Staff, and thermos, crazed. Deafening heat.

Anthem

after Bill Viola

Five thirty a.m., Gary, Indiana.
The heart under knife, its palpitating fibers,
its onyx strands, its cold lard binders,
chalk, mould, mushroom cavities fibrillating faster,
surgeon in the clank of steel, spears,
flies above the cow's fresh mound —

then, mill at dawn, fires keening at its core,
two men step out. Wet and chill
below the canisters of flames and onyx chutes: two men
bright in a scrub plain's hush.
They light small flames for cigarettes they cup,
needles underfoot.

A Poptart™ hits a plate.
Window smudged, chrome toaster specked,
radio drone on a stirring street,
crabgrass, umbrella grass beyond the glass.
Pursed lines above a woman's lip on a cup
lock, clamp, release, dissolve. Then snow.

Romanticism

*In this agon of values, certain freedoms are becoming technically
obsolete. At the same time, freedom, identified with choice as limitless
consumption, elides quickly into the demagogy of the free market.*
— Andrea Brady, "Grief Work in a War Economy"

After giving up full half the cash,
the man walks out on the darkling pier
and watches the buoy flashing green
its shallow water warning.

A minor player: thinking. Gull wing flash.
Antics of a fab-four romp, Juliet readying fast
her lips, crest of an endless wave.
Apes astonied by their slab.

Benzedrine for the Inuit: the man
can see the placard bob,
pinholes pop on the other shore,
his thumb before his eye. Cut.

He is both in the film and author of. Four
red vines — or what's left him of their
shredded selves — whip in the night wind.
He has edited his big scenes out,

doused footage in a sulfite bath, clicked in
place the canister, and authored the review.
Sad Sack in a Walter Mitty Swoon, if he
remembers right, the headline writ.

And now the larger world presses back on him.
Film stock for the sham it is — while, here,
a boat glides by, lit in place where crates
of tractors, bound for Greece,

glow like molten blocks. A tugboat follows
in the trail of foam. In its parapet
a woman in a man's world throttles,
thinks *Knots are up. Knock sense* —

Her son's a scheming narcissist.
Mamá. Yo quiero ser de plata:
lullaby he's repaid her with.
The crates in aft, stacked like skulls,

cubes of glowing cheese. A boy nods
in a Lincoln with his sleeve in shreds —
an ingot fastens to Cortez's hand —
stuck buoy stuttering green. Clear

convention of the stars on high, headlamps
hovering above the man now stumbling on
his feet. So much can go awry. Even film
stock could not matter less, his leading man

now lain so low after giving so much up.
The quay glows, too, in his looping stride;
then he snuffs his steps to turn in late.
Cut. Enough, now, for one night.

Money and God

I

In the country of individuation, I struck out
                                        like a match

for the gravid coast. After the copper fields,
                                        the long loops of city cloverleafs,

the squibs in hillsides spouting the netherworld's flames,
the chrome architraves over gasoline pumps,
                                        signs scrapped up in lead,

and then a lap of colors in the air vault   on the horizon where the black
    spikes spike up

hearing You beside me as a phantom
                                        cursing the radio's warble,

You almost in sight when I turn to the empty seat,

You rigging
                    the fuel pump as it begins to miss,

                                        and then again alone on
lines at burger trains in the chill, sad outposts
Leer & Leak   wobble head for the window rear

after the accordion billboards
Motel 6 a.c. blink   soap ingot and its waxy paper shell

the scent of my striped shirt wagging up from its pit
slubbering of a mechanic in twilight, one night,
the body — *ghastly thing!* — unprepared for reckoning,

after   Eat a Cup of Coffee
                                              a knuckle's scrape against a deli wall
                                              wild turkey   road crossing
                                              swimming air over radiator

                    leg on a train — polyvinylled seat
                              rank john

after the money ran out
after the wire came in
after humilia —

            humid —

                              the homily, end of the nation —

waters   gilded   reared in the sun along a crinoline shore

struck like a match for the sea.

II

And I want to tell You about the houses,
each house of its kind — clapboard or
stucco or timber, Germanic gingerbread, brick or stone,
their blocks cut smooth and
well-fitting, longhouse of mud with its
woven roof —

each had a milky sheen in the afternoon light, whitewash a scrim not of it
but before it, between it and my self, air dunked in milk and the sun —

Or the customs:

small figurines in the front windows winking
straw stuffed in a man's clothes and set on the porches
fiberglass igloos on the lanate lawns

The inhabitants, burly and wild in their cars.
Money
no object.

I saw a woman reach into a parcel of leather with metallic clasps and retrieve
the jangling discourse of our nation
small caterpillars in chrysalides, arrayed
on their ends, and she offered these
to passing motorists, passersby.

A column of eager faces along the roadside at dusk —
A man crying in a park, despite his fierce demeanor —

and I? Done in, missing, hocked at Hocktide. But 'twere
all strange to me. And the hotel too dear.

III

Hell or high water.   *Well, it's the latter. No room for*
the rest of us, let's take the stairs. It's a wallop, learning the delis
won't deliver up here.

Where I had come from, hell *and* high water   fire

and   snow.

                    Sarcophagi picnics — where the lost discussed —

                            Cheating the tax collector —

Yeah you and the ever-loving country said the cowboy, for example,
the spray on his six gallon faint in the sun.
Freesia poured on the tables, dang if it
                            — shut up, we've counted it all and I'm
sick of it now.

Then wheeling out to dominions on the outskirts —
                                red lights, high hopes —
topless skirts' menu: tops, bottoms, *Japanese* or *Russian.*

Interminable billboards —
                    pass the box of Fannie Mae
said Freddie Mac,
                the storm rolled in.

And along that other coast, a longboat carried the crippled souls
bent and twisted into cutouts of the damned, and a wailing trailed
the longboat as it banked beside the man, collector of interest
that he would not confess.

                                    The silo of another moneylender opened,
its wheat now snakes.

                                    A third, awakened by his
servant, found Lucifer
                    and two steeds black before his mill —

                    merchants of the future, sellers of time —

For every *buy high*, a seller's low. You were beside me in the
capit~~ol~~ — al — and then You weren't. Vamoosed like a loan shark
after collect. Denominational oligopsony. Brother Luke
and the double entry. Hermes' fluidity. And so I left.

Now the bright expanse yields up to You.

IV

Radiant sea. I said they were chrysalides, what the woman gave —

The house and its drive faced the sea. The table she'd strutted was meagre but
hewn to endure, with a shiny cloth cover, a checkerboard in red.

Behind her the house glowed milken sheen, a blue like bachelor's buttons
under a tangle of green.

The road along the sea was well tended, loose strife lush on the banks of its
gullies.

I was weary with sleeping-out, sore on my feet. Each town had opened on the
last like commercials. Cars blinking past, a *whshh* and away.

Purgatory, a man by the road said, *was charged for its upbringing, as was
Baudelaire by his stepfather.*

Others had tables, others were tending. Pungent solvents, ochre jellies.
Casts of hands on doilies of silk. Wing covers. Tree frogs singing for tubas.
White curds. One man spread a trunk with bitters and salt.

And I wasn't the only one walking — the cars, the cars in and out, their riders
at hand and in hand of the tables, but the millers like me were sampling on
foot.

I could not not put this between us, too. Your gifts which I fretted, neck
and neck with the costs. To pay Paul, rob

Robert. An impounded car, no more cash by the wire —

I could not not fault You. Turn from your jars. Ochre substan —
sin of the fallen deepest. Shield to the radiant sea.

V

Crows harangue the crowds here, too. Cars break down.

A slippery soot

settles on the beaches

some nights.

An animal tears into a boy's bones

as though they were boxes of sweets;

the deacon fights with his

supervisor,

departs, released.

Flip side, same coin. But knit, a place for each —
Your gifts, within a breach —

From here, on the north cliff, lean-to'd and wanting in the oncoming dusk,
it is difficult to shirk

Your tackle. Right end, left

out. And so I fight —

stars, ready henchmen, pointing —

the sound of water,

down below, lapping —

dive of carrion to the radiant sea.

By

Your banks there would be plenty

so I

turn from them.

Walls of the implacable cliff: dry of the nummary sea.

Depleted Stocks

Figures on a Kylix Attributed to Douris, Athens, 490–480 B.C.

The man holds up three fingers.
The woman holds up four fingers.
She bares a breast.

Trade

Foster & Harding Architects
Architectural Drawings

— a fragment of the scaffolding —

in every variety of style, neatly and promptly executed, for

— writ in the codons, George Mulford Harding to —

Villas, Cottages, Farm Buildings, Churches,

— Daniel Harding Wheeler, Boston to —

or Public Edifices of every kind, including

— Chicago, brawn of the —

Plans, Elevations, Sections and Detail Drawings

— brick & mortar, adenine and guanine —

together with Specifications, Estimates, Contracts, and such
superintendence as may be necessary for the execution of same.

— via Helen Harding Loveland, via May Loveland Wheeler —

Orders from abroad respectfully solicited.

— Ray Barton Wheeler: cedar house on stilts,
the stilts a curve, the helix unzipped —

N. B. — F. & H. will attend to surveying of

— the steel beam, the light seam —

Painting, Plastering, & c, when desired.

— boat house wavering on the north avenue promontory,
ladder up —

Barry Lyndon in Spring Lake, 1985

Benched by the duck pond, he talks about book learning,
swinging his leg on the other, back, forth: diffident in her rage.
And you cannot help overhearing — her tirade, his wheedling replies.
It's the yearning she can't seem to abide. She of slim skirt.

You're done for the day, done and diminished, and the lap
of the pond on its laughable bank won't drown out the shop of his voice.
This man Barry's blind eye for figural blight. The girl reads,
Debtor to your dunner or debtor to death. Book learning.

The LED ticker's impervious to the numbers on its regular lappings.
The girl wads her hair in her fist and releases.
Ditch the story and give us the green.

Greens of the willow, the black maples, the viburnum. Your own bench,
greened in its molds. Green of her t-shirt, green of cold gazes,
Barry goes green under solid regard. Copper pennies, oxide greened.

He's up now and swaying, he's round the pond circling.
Under the browning sky a crow swoops and lands.
He unlooses his watch, he stoops to the bank, he slits with his hands
the shore's green muck. Muck-monger, Barry and his body
follow his hands, slip under the water giving gravity sway. Ducks
shuffle. And the water casts him full back upon shore.

The cylinders of the rotary press impressed the strips from which farthings
were cut, in the Hall in Tyrol. Oh for Chrissakes. Join the human race,
give up the glitz, the snow, what can it be worth, the society you buy?
I don't need Lacroix, you don't need foie gras. Come back to earth
where it's school clothes that call. He: failure of imagination,
grey and skint, that scolds the projected bounty; his: failure to drown.
Despair to denigration, him, now that he's aground. He waves
his loathing back and forth, and the object of it morphs.

You've a prototype in hand, you're an inventor, you've got a transformer
to sell as a toy. Your day's been a hard one courting the *money*,
hoi polloi with muck-hills high as the trees, and in the summer evening
on the still village green it's peace and reprieve that you need,
not a farce of the debtor deranged by his debts, the enabler enraged and the
    pond ducks stirred up. Your briefcase will pillow your head.

Supply the supply side, the slop said.
Power to the people. And the pea brains perk up.
You will have a windfall soon. Lucky numbers: 8, 8, 8, 18.

He has rent his wig. Torn his toupee. The woman turns in green shame.
Barry, gleaming, steps from the green into the lane, gait dogged by honking:
    LeBaron screeched to a halt that lurches, growling, when Barry is by.

I put my hand upon my heart and, there, felt naught but need.
You were in invention's up-tick then, but this you could not know.
Lie on the ties of the eighties track: and this, I did.
No crow swooped which tallied more than contrivèd need.

Song of the Deserving

Guy on the street's got a Fluxus bird for sale;
Whaddaya want for it? I say, but his head's in a pail.
For me to know and for you to find out.

You're screaming in the driveway I scratched up your car;
There's a guy watching, but his take on you's bizarre:
For me to know and for you to find out.

I tried to touch your earlobe but you winced at my touch;
Late morning ferry has a drip in its clutch. What did you expect?
For me to know and for you to find out.

Ever since yesterday the ringing in my ears
Won't let me rest, so I came over here.
For me to know and for you to find out.

It's all in the delivery, the comic told the class,
But Bobby Bradley raised his hand: *why, jackass?* —
For me to know and for you to find out.

I thought I had what I needed in this trailer out on 9,
Lots of French-milled handsoap and a barrel full of wine.
For me to know and for you to find out.

In the woods this morning three wild turkeys followed me
Up to Cushing's Corner and then hit the key of C,
For me to know and for you to find out.
Don't you know,
For me to know and for you to find out.

Port in the Airport

This, the air traffic control in its cell;
this, the mechanic Jorge *en carte*,
Dzvinia pecking keys by the red hots display,
eyeing runway and sun, and orange, and lee-

way to the causeway on the underbelly of
  — the man with the wad.
He pockets the change. Condiment
island. Weaves, then: *Scheiss.* Not a syllable alike.

> *Skeletal garnet, truss trove joint*
> *Wooden belly iron back fire in th' hole*

and the semblance of cash, the shock of true bills.
The sun pours on orange cones a glory, wet.
Esther in her *mantilla.* Jose *can* see, no, say,
no — sop, amid a skirtless room's stalls, the

spray sprung from dicks there aswing. Bob sings
despite the irk of his friends on the walk-
way to the pod where the sun doesn't reach. . . .
He was a railroad — killed a mile —

True love, *true love,* stunned polity! Beth
Ann wheels the cart to cargo and riles,
stoops, flops a duffle on Fendi on trunk —
liquid simulacra, *consider the radi-ance — or -al —*

> *— There was a little one-eyed gunner sang*
> *"Catch a falling sputnik, put it in a matchbox,*

send it to the U.S.A. They'll be glad to get it,
very glad to get it — " José, Jorge.
The child in the smoking lounge leans into legs,
screws gun arm to elbow on X-ray Baldeen.

Toward Autumn

> matted to a dank thing
> twist of Cape Cod kindling

the shredder   the sprinkler   Symbionese Army —

fall, and a wren has a glossy page clamped into its beak.
The wren balks, the wren pops the clamp and clamps again,
the woman and the machine gun in the sedum browning,
bit wind the leaves loosening, the fairy rose swaying,
a whipping of water at the baby oak.

> The leaf, its nematode.
> Cat wary of water, and —

the glossy page, does it predate the summer's dry season?
A reason must I have to return and find one? The green

> hose snaked by the rose of Sharon,
> spiraea bobbing fronds in the breeze.

Overtaxed Lament

The ungendered (it, say) told itself it did not want a superstore, did not want
   superficial coverage,
preferred the hardware store, the deli, the bagel store, shoe repair, and that it
   could not expect to find oranges at the hardware — but this hardware store
   had only sex, and shelter, and love, little in the way of art or empathy or
   curiosity, and so be it, it argued despite its desire for all to have all without
moving, without shopping, the breast *there* and not episodic, satiety not a
   sometime thing.

Trudging store to store. Exorbitant costs withheld, it moving patiently in lines
   toward cashiers like cattle. Calculate the costs in time. Consider the
   superstore.
Lucretius and his atoms, rising. *Trop cher.*
The guest who brings the uninvited. Shit!
Gift inveigling gift.

This man or woman, this *it* with hair, bipedal, consuming pork and romaine
   and the filaments of what extrudes from bulbs,
it hadn't been thinking straight from square one.
The train compartment and the local commuters. The swaying train man, his
   paunch. Sharing a seat, say, an expense of the utmost. It held in its hand
the freight of costly compassion and reeled. *I* reeled.

God who edges closer, nose-whistling as he/she/it breathes. Cost of. Dint of.
   Open exchange in the whim-whams of want.

"Worth the trouble," Herodotus may have said of Helen. It thought the eye of
   the beholder might know this alone, it wanting Herodotus to weigh its own
   procurements (nuts and nails) from its hardware spree. Roof deep and dry
   and
wide. Overhung by an olive tree.

The Debtor in the Convex Mirror

— after Quentin Massys, c. 1514

He counts it out. By now from abroad there are shillings and real —
Bohemian silver fills the new coins — but his haul is gold, écu au soleil,
excelente, mostly: wafers thin and impressed with their marks, milled
new world's gold the Spanish pluck or West African ore Portugal's

slaves sling. The gold wafers gleam in their spill by the scale.
Calm before gale: what bought a sack a century before almost
buys a sack now; the Price Revolution's to come. A third of a mason's —
a master one's — day's wage funds the night's wine, Rhine, for his crew

after a big job wraps up. As for dried herring, his day's wage would buy
fifteen mille for a big do; his workers, just nine — 18 stroo. Calm in his
commerce is the businessman, and his wife, their disheveled shelves:
she turns a page; her hands are in God but her gaze is on ange-nobles

and pearls, weights and gold rings — one florin in pan, one in his hand.
What sync they are in: calm their regard, luxe, volupté leur mien.
Fur trimmings on jackets, gemstones on fingers — while the
debtor in the mirror has spent what he has on the red hat he's in.

Prayer book illumined: luxury *that*, and to ignore: only more.
Calmed by the calculation of interest, though the figure's been
clear for a good quarter hour, the moneylender withholds it and waits:
the debtor is better with fuzz in his head. In truth, *he*'s distressed: cares

like the shield impressed in the écu dint the meet of his brow
beneath the red hat. What's he reading? Or faking? Caught in the
curve of an office's alarm, an anti- to crime, a drugstore's big boon
long centuries to come, the debtor — about to receive knell to what

peace he might otherwise recall — worries his page. Ability for
reading silently may not be his; the lender's wife puts him to shame,
though the shame in this is the least of his shames. In the yard
beyond her waits one of his lienors for the gold of another.

Schoolmarms ahoy. Scrap history, the parable, the prayer of the
illustrated hours she trembles to hold. He's got his gold, she's mes-
merized or not by its sheen, the debtor's lost to our reflecting of him —
but it's without, a measurement is made — a figure's gesture on the

gravitate street, the fury of a face *in its face*, behind the door ajar, the
fingers of the lienor demarcating fast the size of a peck or a pecker
not so. *The debt is as large as a giant's back turning, large as*
a vulcanic forge. And

                    fragment of the debt imbursed —

                                        size of its toy —

intense regard.

Fume individually, fume

borrower, clipper, catcher, coiner, getter, grabber, hoarder, loser, lover, raiser,
    spender, teller, thirster —

                                scrivener lays out upon collateral, but
what has the red-hat? Zero

                                        and then sum.

So *here* you are.   Master.

These ideas,
said Friedländer, were "common possession, freebooty, fair game."

A painting by Jan van Eyck eighty years before Massys', glimpsed
and described in Milan but now lost, was its model: banker and wife;

the portrait of Giovanni Arnolfini in a red hat not unlike Massys' debtor and,
a year earlier, Arnolfini and his wife at their marriage, we know. In the latter,

the self van Eyck daubed in its own convex mirror (one of four figures),
affixed like a crucifix on the backdrop of wall, rides the conjoined hands

as a charm. But nothing foreshadowed the hand of your own.
Your painter's (nineteen, set off for Rome with the jewel of his art)

hand in the gem of its bulge, the hand the pope pronto kissed
with commission — a job, you note, never come through.

Genre derives from the devotional: beauty and *ange* on one side,
deformity by vice on the other, or so said Friedländer. He found the wife's
          gaze

full of dispirit, "lofty sadness." She and her husband are yes tight-lipped.
The palm of the hand, like the open mouth, were Massys' registries

of emotionality, he wrote, but the souls in this painting have neither.
Sentimentally, it *pleases* Massys "to feel sorrow, and grief takes on

mild forms." Worry's otherwise: Massys' St. Anthony, elsewhere,
tempted by courtesans, peaks his brows — wild, broken peaks! — same as

the moneylender's debtor. So much for effects, effects of Massys,
virtuoso, whose pyrotechnics, "new wine poured into old bottles,"

welled "from a kind of nervous energy — in any event, not from the heart."
"*The antithesis of artist*" (Friedländer, still): this, the debtor to Leonardo,

to Van Eyck, may well have known, knowledge well welling his brows in the
mirror the moneylender ignores. *My guide in these matters is your self,*

your own soul permeable by beauty,   and mine not,
not even by the swirling of facts, leveling —

                              how far, indeed,

can the soul *swim out through the eyes and still return safely to its nest?*
That it be

possible

                    I cannot leave. Though around me, and the art,

I fail.

                              Thérèse

was the lookout. She watched the cashier in the convex mirror, and I
watched Jean Shrimpton on the point-of-purchase long before it had
its name.　　Thérèse:

careful, Catholic, pregnant and smoking.

lips　　　　　　　　　　　　lipstick

I took the

cylinder in my fingers and slipped it to Christmas. Thérèse: to the racks,
Seventeen, Tiger Beat. A few moments more and we'd be through the door.

Maybe it was *in* the painter's hand, *out for a dole*
— so close with Clement's promise! —
that he sought a soul.

And these coins, fragments of a web —

Mary sat and did not labor, despite her Martha's sting.

It's still, tonight. The peepers, out, self-
restrain.
Sometimes a welling up: I've lost

thought in images. Night: a blank.
The stars just stars.
The sternies prick like whin.
Kid's bicycle on its rim, under the road lamp chill
as ice.
A soul could be blank as these bald things.
Are blank. Or so we thought.

So this much we have: banker and wife, waist-up at table, she
with her prayer book watching the gold coins spill on the surface

before us. What we see in their clothes is the waist-cinch:
her red seamy bodice, his jacket, furred collars and cuffs.

Behind them, just two shelves: account books and objects —
then, out a window or door, two figures obscured but for

faces and heads, one forefinger and thumb in a U.
In the fore of the table, a diverging mirror, gold frame,

askew. And, by his reflected place, we see, we viewers,
sitting right where we are, a red-hatted man who holds

a book to his chin as though he is sunning. Rather,
he's reading — or trying, by the fold in his brow.

Real light, long, late-day, slants through the window
above him where a steeple's filigree's revealed. And that's all.

Most agree the red-hatted reader's the painter; it matches
his portrait from Wiericx's engraving. The clothing's

outdated, the banker's wife's bodice derives from the portrait
Van Eyck did of his wife Margaret in that weird hornèd hat.

And Saint Eligius, patron of goldsmiths, converter of Antwerp,
in Christus' scene, had a curved mirror turned toward outdoors.

Copies of Massys come later. They drop the debtor, insert a
messenger. Imitators of Massys update

                                  the coins.

Not
          that the convex tondo, inside of a painting, was not a dozen a dime —
                    not just Massys, not just Van Eyck, it was *in the wind* blowing,
               in Brabant, in Ghent, Bruges, Anvers, through the Burgundy hold,
                              fresh off a pub's haul and into the workshop,
                    popping up through the guilds   ghastly cliché it was then.

But
        we get   ahead   rewind   to the Lowlands   begin.

Astonishing city. A rube, let's say Charles, onions in sacks slung on his
mule's back, he a standout in his coarse sayette, enters this Antwerp,
inhales as he draws near the docks. Gulls swoop; three Fuggers, capitalists,

in wool dickedinnen, speaking abreast in deliberate tread, stop him
cold crossing his path. Street stalls of changers, merchants with money;
crates unloading — fish, sugar — by Spaniards and Danes;

dragomen emitting unrecognizable tongues: such swirl over Charles
in our genre-esque scene. In the movie, we'd hear the THX *clok*,
hooves in their wary trades forth. What little Charles knows of this place

he has heard at the fairs in the mediant towns outlying the western Ypres.
On the way, there'd been Ghent, its self-satisfied sense. Talk there of
trade throttled by this guild or that, trade nip-and-tuck against Bruges':

Antwerp, said an oiler in Deinze, *up-and-comer is it, if you want one*
that is. Hub of all nations, market of kings. Nothing there, either,
to stand in the way of a man with ambition or a star in his bush.

No, if you're smart, you'll go there and quick. Charles had nodded
and drunk from his mug, but the notion then planted by the man
took root. Now, in the pitch of the persons, in the roil of the merchants,

Charles sees there the commerce: purposeful, restive, serene —
a trade's un-self-consciousness, a self-sufficiency in such —
and Charles is impressed. His own small purse, pendant in his

pocket, feels slight but sufficient to one.

Anna Bijns, the young lady
says to him not three days later. She's forthright as a slip, and at once
he wants the pocket fuller, a past that's not his. A girl of means, she —

she could show him her whole shelf of books, her writing-room, her
verses that denounce the psalm-sop, Luther. *Like his sins are*
worse than ours, she'll say, to those more worthy of answer.

"Town common to all nations," Guicciardini later wrote of the city.
"First 'capitalist' center . . . in the modern sense," wrote Chlepner.
When Charles and Massys shared Antwerp its reign had just begun;

each week brought scores of foreigners, folded in like butter,
out to let a household kept kempt in local fashion, clean,
its Dinanderie in order and its linens boiled and hung.

Down Gulden Street, the house that's held by the Hanseatic corn
market; across the way, the square that will become, in a score of
years, the world's first stock exchange — shops, fragrant with

Portuguese spices, beckon with the latest haul. The merchant
moneylender leans to the obsolescence of his coins — the paper
debts he trades more in leave gold to the unconjoined, sole

debtors like this painter worrying his paper text. *Livre tournois,*
the French would call them, units of money valued at a Roman
pound, and *livre, book:* not the first time the two're confused.

Charles, counting his ducats, catches a red hat from the *coin*
of his eye, costume of a century before: it's Massys he sees.
The painter's off to work in the salt-crusted air, preparing

— away from the *shadow of a city, siphon,* you wrote, of the life
of the studio —

                                              his self to be seen.

New York tonight
                         boils in its heat wave. The sidewalks
burn soles. Haze like a coat warms up the ones out.   Prague

floods.

        The market's in side-flip. Each day doubling back
                                              the day before,
lobbing,
the stalk that holds coral bells tracing its arbitrary round. Perhaps
the U on the street
                         is a score.

                                        Principal export:

ask Bernays, *he'll* know.   Buy low.

The painter in the mirror wants privacy, not this call that invades
the reading of a book. Your own looked out at us, but mine, *Massys* —
disingenuous, masquerading, stressed and damp — doesn't; weightier

things on his mind he's got not. But he only pretends to absorption.
It's we who discern the privacy he wants, we who can see
what he lacks. It's as though we're instructed to trust the lender,
his own fix being more, well, *sequestered.*
The last century mined focus as a notion, and even here in Manhattan,
a delirium of sorts swabbing its streets,
we tread with the intensity of hounds,
plugged into our earpiece conjointments, or collecting loose change
off of cuffs. Massys' grimace underdramatizes our lot.

thassright, that's what makes genres —

pink ribbon, blue bob —
thaler for the watched fob.

No, thalers   come later.

Not much, you prig.

Later enough.

So the grasping soul is unredeemed. *Freak accident —*
yeah, guy goes up a hill in thorns, ends up on a stick.
Not quite, not impaled, more tacked up.   *Yeah.*
And the grasping soul goes clean.

Maybe it's our internalness
we're stuck on.
                                O Captain Me, O Consciousness.
The soul *negotiates* its right of way,

                                O consciousness,

but not without a bargain struck with*out*. Why all
or nothing, is what Charles thinks, watching the painter disappear

O Captain Me

                                in a costume fit to paint. After all,
Charles doesn't know the painter's
destination.

                                In a cloud left by dusty wheels, he

                                O captain me, o

hears a boy call *natura naturata! Red (Flemish) herring! —*
and wells with tears. Impossible   *o consciousness*
that this he heard, silt eyes silt ears

                Copper's up

in an older voice, murmuring, away — strange songs of spring that reach the
    rube in worsted wraps, wheels clattering about his self, while each breath,
    immarginate,

clangs to differentiate its action from the world's.

O captain me.
Sad country sack, negotiant, kneels in the dust to pray.

                              He crams so much in, Massys. *And then I reached*
that time in life when, all my spices scattered, every story turned

                                             lapsarian.

Every surface filled with hardware, pots, jetons — a collector's box —
the world impresses back, impresses with a shield or beast or profile of a noble
     sort —
the same impressions, though the edges of each coin be irregular and bent —
it being half a century before die standardized.
And even then, this penny black with chewing gum, that one having seen
the inside of a shoe, this none but a banker's roll — the analogy

goes grim. Or is it metaphor, what we strive for, we

poets. Bookmakers with the odds of slugs.

                              We don't need paintings or / doggerel
                              and on this too you're true.

The man hand-making his U in the yard
knows Massys's a kite-man, bad risk, a debtor. All glow and show

and then off

world, world, world   with him. Each
time
intent to aliment not only he but they

world

what comes his way   gives way.

Even tonight, here, stampede of slugs

in all that enters here, in
pages strewn, in air report and digit-pulse: *his way*. The debtor does not know
his debt to the skittering city. The bank of birds up a skyscraper's flank.
Patience of his creditors. What does a trust in surfaces ensure but faith that
the surfaces move?

Blue surroundings. Your nose, welling in the car mirror's arc —
my own in the hubcap hull —

What is this but an arrangement of figures on an open field?
But *they overlap* — and this is the *heart*, despite Friedländer,

the heart of the bind of the debtor: a debt becoming due.
Inveigling the day to take orders from *him* — such a ray from the
cathedral, still in construction, for which Massys' metalwork
is said to encircle a well — the red-hatted man pretends.

The soul encumbers what no other soul knows? Think again.
The mirror lies between two scales — one banker's, one maker's —

and Massys is but writ on its glass. It's the man in the courtyard,
the jig up with fingers, who'll reckon the dark fundamentals

once the weigh-ins are done. And the world impresses him, too.

The *world* overlaps them indentures them both.

                                        Car door bangs. Dark Brooklyn, dark
clattering night.

                        Though the lineage's strong for the sons of moneylenders,

daughters   don't carry.   They get the short end. *The debtor's excuses*

                                                                are many

for the false fealty of her deals.
                                                                79

Adept at outline, Friedländer meant. Ready angle of the couple's arms, echo of the angle in the glass. Her limpid face lit sole. Debtor's histrionics, a painter's joke shallow as they go.

Car door creaks its opening, back for a pack
of cigarettes. Side mirror loose, door slam. Wheeled overland

            from Venice
the Venetian goods — and cotton, from Levant —
are writ up
      (in the noon sun and portside)

   and certified lading.
The paper suffices for sugar and salt.

Acknowledgments

Many texts have contributed to—and, in some cases, have been robbed for—these poems. Those that have not been cited within the body of the book include Geoffrey Chaucer's "Complaint to His Purse"; *The Book of Common Prayer*, 1979 edition; John Suckling's "Love and Debt Alike Troublesome"; William Wordsworth's "The Laborer's Noonday Hymn"; the journal *American Speech* (Summer 1994); Terry Eagleton's "Let's Go Through It One More Time," from the *Times Literary Supplement* (October 31, 1997, issue 4935); Mennonite traditional text; Emily Dickinson's "Fame is a fickle food," #1659; articles by Frank Bruni and Elizabeth Becker ("Charity Is Told It Must Abide by Antidiscrimination Laws") and by Evelyn Nieves ("Calls for Change in an Ancient Occupation") in the *New York Times*, July 11, 2001; Solomon 8 in *The New Oxford Annotated Bible*; Federico García Lorca's "Cancion Tonta"; Sir Theodore Martin's "The Debate of the Body and Soul"; Ezra Pound's *Cantos*; Jacques Le Goff's *Your Money or Your Life*; Lewis Hyde's *The Gift*; anonymous riddles cited in Tom Paulin's *The Faber Book of Vernacular Verse*; James Buchan's *Frozen Desire: An Inquiry into the Meaning of Money*; Fernand Braudel's *Afterthoughts on Material Civilization and Capitalism*; Marc Shell's *Money, Language, and Thought*; Rowan D. Williams's essay, "Between Politics and Metaphysics: Reflections in the Wake of Gillian Rose," in *Modern Theology* (11:1 January 1995); work by the economist John H. Munro; W. P. Blockmans's essay, "The Formation of a Political Union, 1300–1600," in *History of the Low Countries*, edited by Blom and Lamberts; Jean Baudrillard's *The Accursed Share: An Essay on General Economy*; John Ashbery's "Self-Portrait in a Convex Mirror" and "Definition of Blue"; Kathleen Jamie's "Jocky in the Wilderness"; William Shakespeare's *Merchant of Venice*; B. S. Chlepner's "Economic Development of Belgium" in *Belgium*, edited by Jan-Albert Goris; Max Friedländer's *Early Netherlandish Painting*; *A History of Private Life: Passions of the Renaissance*, edited by Philippe Aries and Georges Duby; Emile Cammaerts's *A History of Belgium*; Elaine Pagels's *The Origin of Satan*; *Getting and Spending: European and American Consumer Societies in the*

Twentieth Century, edited by Strasser, McGovern, and Judt; Jonathan Williams's *Money: A History*; and David Standish's *The Art of Money*.

Poems in *Ledger* have appeared in the *Yale Review, London Review of Books, St. Anne's Review, Mississippi Review, Conjunctions, New American Writing, Jacket, Poetry Review, Conduit, Skanky Possum, The Gig, Verse, Crowd, Open City, Poetry International, Five Fingers Review, and POOL*. "Short Shrift" also appeared in *re: Chapbook 4*, edited by Beth Andersen. *The Debtor in the Convex Mirror* was published as a chapbook by Wild Honey Press in 2004.

Many thanks, for general direction, to Roger Ferlo and Nina Frost; for helpful readings and editings, to Nate Dorward, Randolph Healy, Steve Martin, J. D. McClatchy, Claudia Rankine, Elena Rivera, Denise Tanyol, and David Trinidad; for faith and patience, to Bill Clegg; for manuscript assistance and preparation, to Preeti Sodhi; and for all of the above, as ever, to Philip Furmanski.

THE IOWA POETRY PRIZE &
EDWIN FORD PIPER POETRY AWARD WINNERS

1987

Elton Glaser, *Tropical Depressions*

Michael Pettit, *Cardinal Points*

1988

Bill Knott, *Outremer*

Mary Ruefle, *The Adamant*

1989

Conrad Hilberry, *Sorting the Smoke*

Terese Svoboda, *Laughing Africa*

1990

Philip Dacey, *Night Shift at the Crucifix Factory*

Lynda Hull, *Star Ledger*

1991

Greg Pape, *Sunflower Facing the Sun*

Walter Pavlich, *Running near the End of the World*

1992

Lola Haskins, *Hunger*

Katherine Soniat, *A Shared Life*

1993

Tom Andrews, *The Hemophiliac's Motorcycle*

Michael Heffernan, *Love's Answer*

John Wood, *In Primary Light*

1994

James McKean, *Tree of Heaven*

Bin Ramke, *Massacre of the Innocents*

Ed Roberson, *Voices Cast Out to Talk Us In*

1995

Ralph Burns, *Swamp Candles*

Maureen Seaton, *Furious Cooking*

1996

    Pamela Alexander, *Inland*

    Gary Gildner, *The Bunker in the Parsley Fields*

    John Wood, *The Gates of the Elect Kingdom*

1997

    Brendan Galvin, *Hotel Malabar*

    Leslie Ullman, *Slow Work through Sand*

1998

    Kathleen Peirce, *The Oval Hour*

    Bin Ramke, *Wake*

    Cole Swensen, *Try*

1999

    Larissa Szporluk, *Isolato*

    Liz Waldner, *A Point Is That Which Has No Part*

2000

    Mary Leader, *The Penultimate Suitor*

2001

    Joanna Goodman, *Trace of One*

    Karen Volkman, *Spar*

2002

    Lesle Lewis, *Small Boat*

    Peter Jay Shippy, *Thieves' Latin*

2003

    Michele Glazer, *Aggregate of Disturbances*

    Dainis Hazners, *(some of) The Adventures of Carlyle, My Imaginary Friend*

2004

    Megan Johnson, *The Waiting*

    Susan Wheeler, *Ledger*